When Marguritha Ann's Period Began

Written by
Dr. Lillian M. Harris

Copyright Page:
All Rights Reserved
Copyright © 2008 by Dr. Lillian M. Harris

No part of this book may be reproduced or transmitted, downloaded, distributed, reverse engineered, or stored in or introduced into any information storage and retrieval system, in any form or by any means, including photocopying and recording, whether electronic or mechanical, now known or hereinafter invented without permission in writing from the publisher.

ISBN: 978-0-692-83426-8

Illustrator: Andrea Pollard

Published in the United States
by Writer's Tablet Publishing Agency
Marietta, Georgia
www.WritersTabletAgency.com

For inquiries, please contact Dr. Lillian at BooksbyDrLil@gmail.com

DEDICATION

Dedicated to my beautiful daughter, Alena Marne',
with all my love every day!

ACKNOWLEDGEMENT

I would like to thank some of the extraordinary people in my life because their love and support made this book possible. My husband, Charlton, Sr., supported my vision and helped to secure an awesome publishing company, Writers Tablet, LLC. My children, Maurice, Alena, and Charlton, Jr., continuously inspire me to be creative. My mom, Maudesta, and my siblings, Eddie, Lory, and Sean, have always been my biggest cheerleaders. In fact, a few years after I wrote this book for my daughter, my sister (and soror), Lory, borrowed the book to have "the talk" with her daughter, Kala. Lory was one of the first people to encourage me to publish the book.

My cousin Talisha also used the book for her daughters and wanted to see it published. When my daughter-in-law, Dachele, found out about this book, she asked that I please have it published in time enough for her daughter, my granddaughter, Maurie.

Thank you to my sister-cousin Michelle and my sister/soror cousin Kesha whom I can always count on for laughs and great conversations.

A special thanks to my friend and soror, Dr. Jacqueline Miller, for your input and expertise.

I have shared this book with countless family and friends, and they all shared the same sentiment, please publish! Through the love and support from family and friends, I am grateful to finally present this book to the world.

Her mom had a long talk with her one day
And this is what she had to say...

"The time has come for you to know
More about your body as you continue to grow

Things will change, and you must be prepared
We're having this talk so you won't be scared"

Marguritha Ann's attention began to pique
She sat quietly as her mom continued to speak,

"Your experiences might be like mine since you're my daughter
But the changes don't come in any particular order"

"One day you will begin to have a little pain in your chest,
But it will come and go as you develop your breasts

When you feel like this, you must let me know
So I can make sure you're healthy as you continue to grow"

Marguritha Ann was excited to know
That soon her breasts would begin to grow

She looked at her mom with eyes sparkling like stars
And asked if they could go shopping for her very first bra

Her mom simply replied, "We will go one day,
But listen closely for now; I have more to say"

"You will begin to grow hair in other places
Like under your arms and down-below spaces"

"Sometimes you just won't feel your best
You'll just want to relax and get some rest

When you feel like this, you must let me know
So I can make sure you're healthy as you continue to grow"

"One day your tummy will have some pain
Not because you're hungry; it's not the same

Below your stomach you'll feel sharp aches, pain, and little jerks
You might feel more tired and your head might hurt"

"I remember that feeling," Marguritha Ann said
"It's like when I had the flu and had to stay in bed"

Her mom replied, "That might be true
Sometimes you might feel like you have the flu"

"There is a good reason why you'll feel this way
Your menstrual cycle will begin in just a few days

Remember... when you feel like this, you must let me know
So I can make sure you're healthy as you continue to grow"

"The menstrual cycle has a common nickname
It's called a 'period', but it means the same"

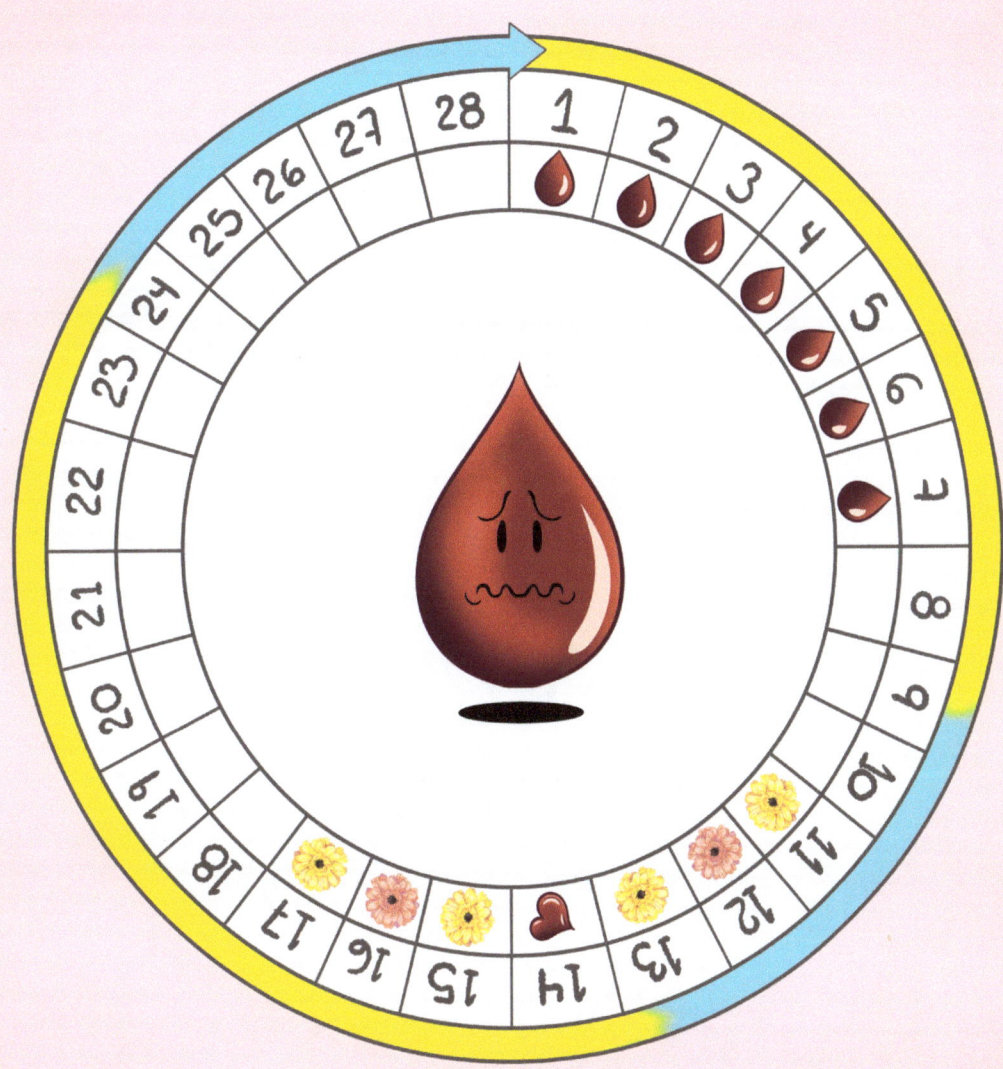

"You see, your body has ovaries that produce eggs
And one is released on day fourteen of every twenty-eight days"

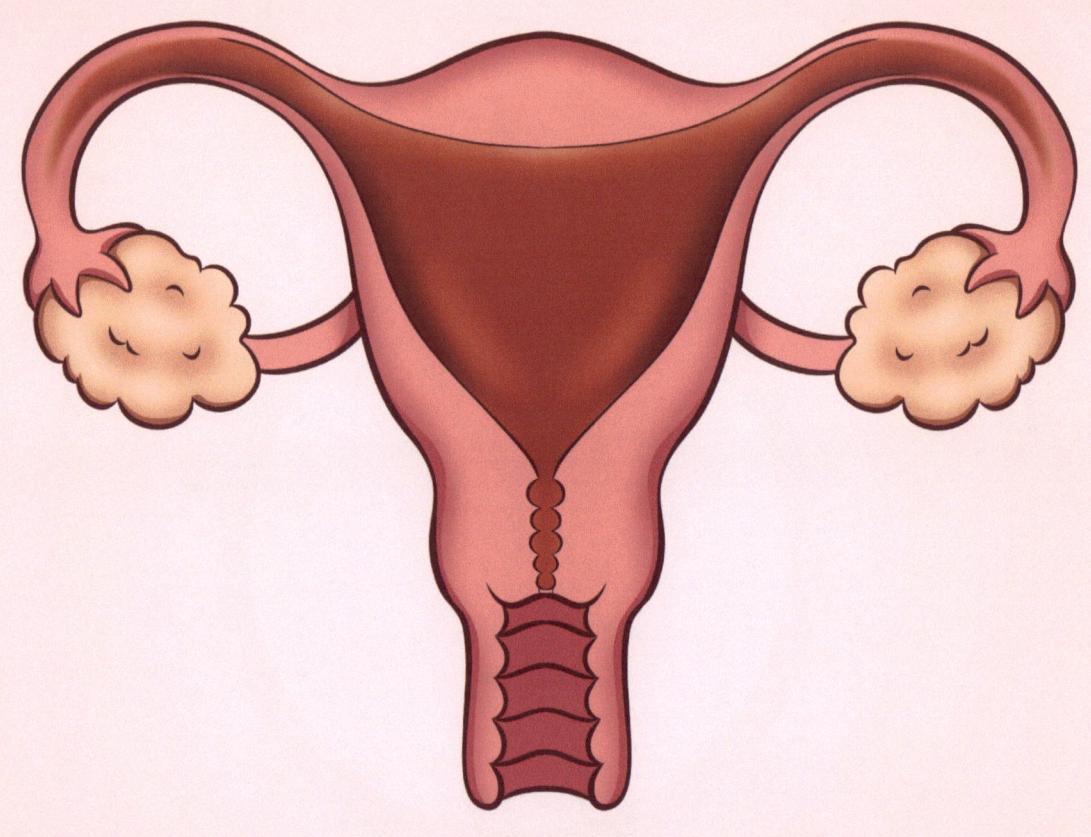

"Look at the female reproductive system for a better view,
Of how these changes will occur when it happens to you"

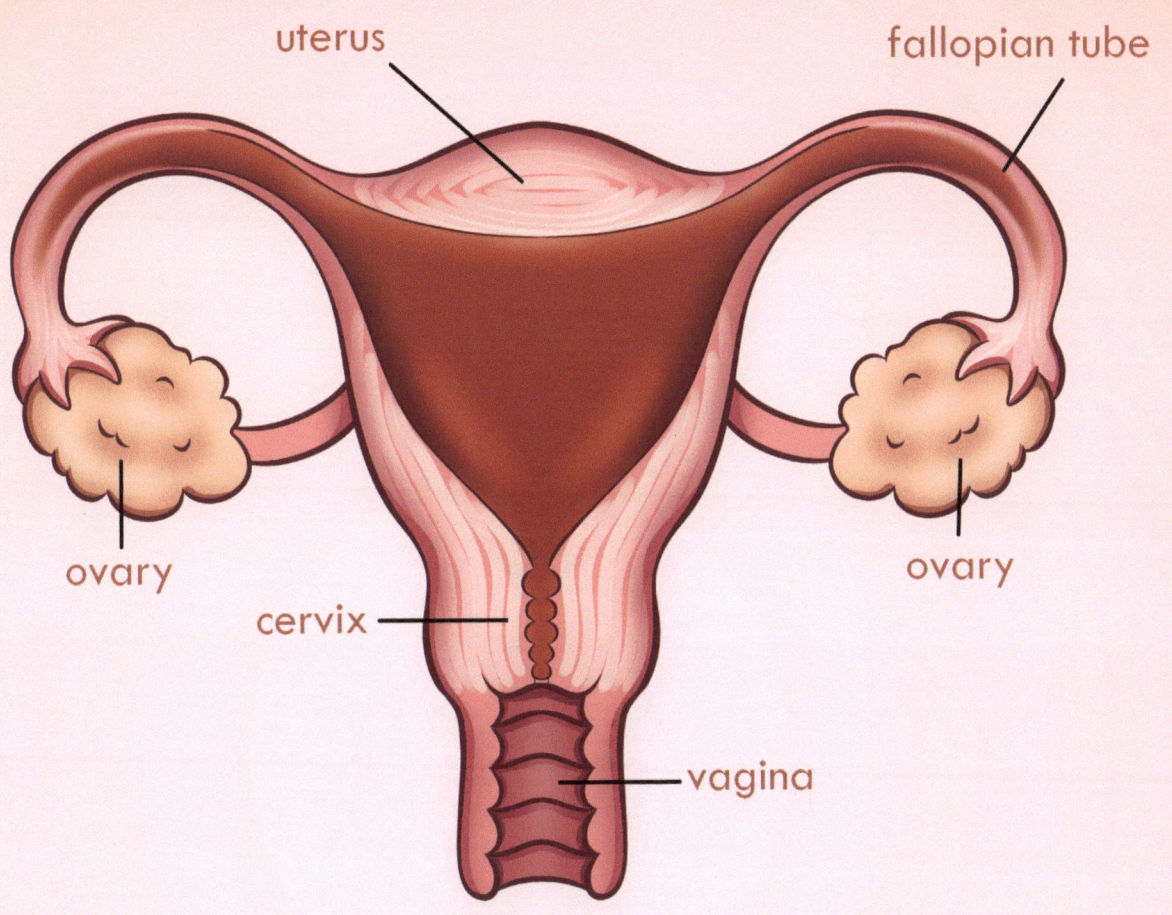

"The ovary is the home for your eggs,
It sends one out on the fourteenth day

The egg travels to the fallopian tube,
And for the next fourteen days it continues to move

Into the uterus that's shaped like a funnel,
Then through the cervix, a very small tunnel"

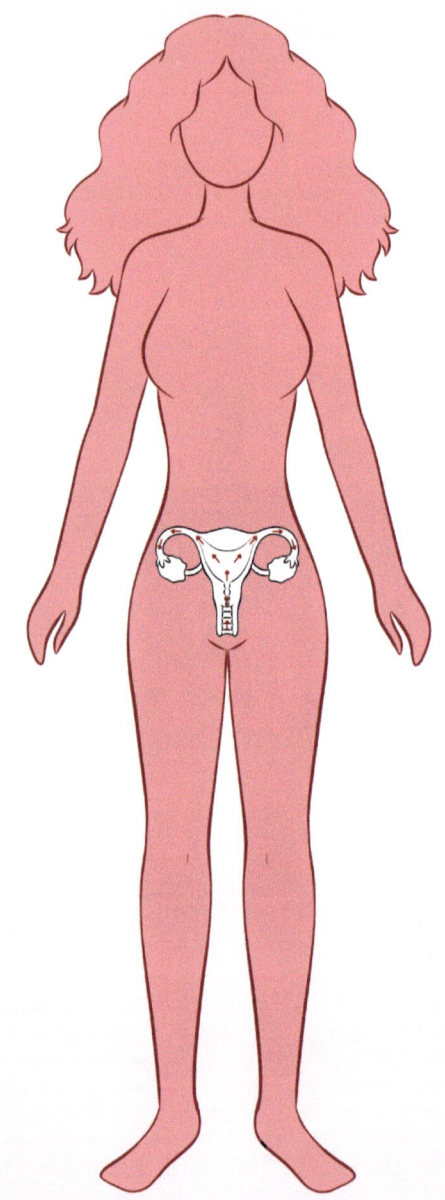

"The egg is too small for the human eye to view,
But it causes a lot of pain as it tries to squeeze through"

"When it comes through the vagina, you begin to bleed
But don't be afraid,
it's blood and fluid that your body no longer needs"

"Wow," said Marguritha Ann,
"sounds like the period does a lot
Is a period like at the end of a sentence?
Does it leave a small dot?"

"Your blood flow could be a little or a lot,
Like a few tablespoons or just a few spots"

Your period will last about five days
from beginning to end,
Then your body goes through the process
for more eggs to descend

Now you'll need to be prepared to prevent a big mess,
And it begins with supplies as you start to dress"

There are a few options to help you prepare
To keep your clothes clean and protect your underwear

Most girls choose a pad to wear
It comes in different sizes and sticks right inside your underwear"

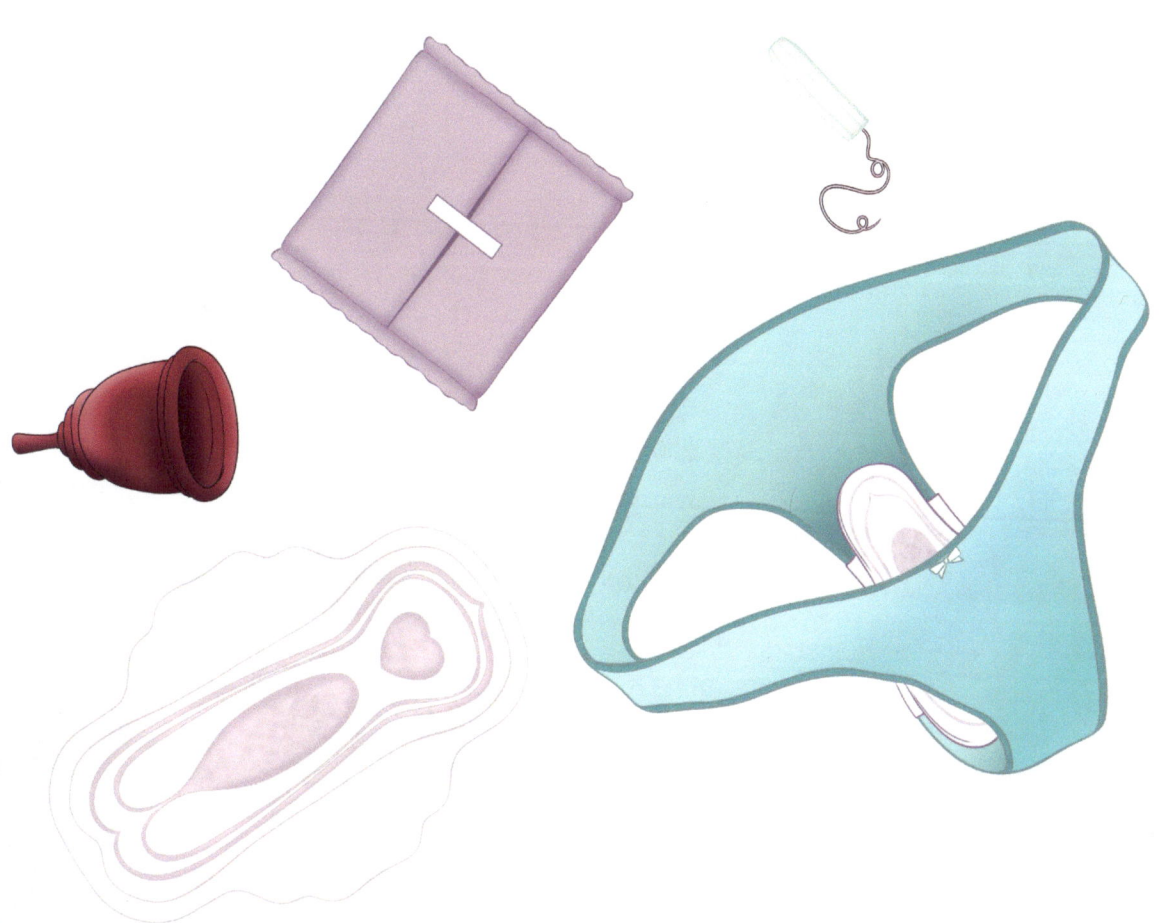

"On how much fluid you flow
when your period begins
Here are some samples for you to see
How short or long and thin or thick a pad can be"

"Change it often to prevent a rash
Fold the used one up, wrap it in tissue,
and put it in the trash"

"There's just one more thing for you to know
To take care of your body as you continue to grow

You must freshen up throughout the day
when your period begins
And take a nice long shower as each day ends"

"That's all for now, and I hope you know
More about your body as you continue to grow

But always remember that I'm right by your side
To answer your questions as they arise"

Marguritha Ann felt safe and secure
Knowing how her body was about to mature

For the next few months,
Marguritha Ann's body began to change
Much like her mom had already explained

She remembered to let her mom know
About all the changes as she continued to grow

Then one day, just out of the blue
The start of her period finally came through

She followed all the steps her mom had explained
And went to talk to her mom about how she had changed

As she told her mom the exciting news
One thing had her terribly confused

"I was wondering," said Marguritha Ann, "as I got dressed
Now that my period has started, where are my breasts?"

Her mom smiled and said,
"My sweet little daughter, Remember the changes
don't come in any particular order"

Marguritha Ann was relieved to be reminded of that
Because all of her friends had breasts but she was still flat

"You're a late bloomer," said Mom, "but that's okay,
Late bloomers take longer but they still bloom in their own way

Your questions are important, Marguritha Ann,
You can always ask me anything and I will answer if I can"

"I do have another question!" shouted Marguritha Ann,
"Why do we have periods anyway?
And once it starts how many years will it stay?"

Mom looked at her with a glimmer in her eyes
Gave her a big hug and simply replied,